Interviews and text by Jordan Paramor
Blue is managed by Daniel Glatman for Intelligent Music Management Ltd.

First published 2003 by **Contender Books**
Contender Books is a division of
The Contender Entertainment Group
48 Margaret Street
London W1W 8SE

www/contendergroup.com/books

This edition published **2003**

1 3 5 7 9 10 8 6 4 2

ISBN 1 84357 073 4

Production: **Sasha Morton**
Design: **Button One to One**
Printed in Italy by **Officine Grafiche DeAgostini srl**

Picture Credits

PA Photos: 6, 19, 28, 57, 59 (2)
Rex Features: 19, 21, 29, 31, 35, 36-7, 38 (2), 39 (2), 43, 45, 46-47, 50, 51, 59 (2)
Alpha: 30, 42, 44 (2), 45
Ken Goff Photos: 59

All other images (including front and back cover) courtesy of
Virgin International / Intelligent Music Management

Blue

The Official Annual 2004

JORDAN PARAMOR

Hello and welcome to the fantastic Blue annual 2004. If you're a big Blue fan, you probably think you know pretty much everything there is to know about the lads. But here they reveal all about their favourite events of their previous year, you can find out which Blue gang you'd be best suited to, tread the path to true Blue love and find out what's in store for the lads in the year ahead with our horoscope special. Get stuck in!

→ Lee

Full name: Lee Ryan
DOB: 17/6/1983
Height: 5' 11"
From: South East London
Hair: Blonde
Eyes: Green / Blue
Star sign: Gemini
Siblings: One sister
Favourite TV show: *Only Fools and Horses*
Favourite film: *Stand By Me*
Favourite sweets: Cakes like Tiramisu, Banoffee Pie, Mississippi Mud Pie and sorbets
Most romantic thing he's ever done: Cooked dinner for a girl
Favourite flavour of crisps: Doesn't like them!
Favourite Blue song: 'Long Time'
First single ever bought: 'How Come, How Long' by Stevie Wonder and Babyface
Favourite catchphrase: 'Spanish', as in 'Spanish Waiter' for 'later'

→ Duncan

Full name: Duncan Matthew James
DOB: 7/4/1979
Height: 5' 11"
From: Devon and Dorset
Hair: Light Brown / Blonde
Eyes: Blue
Star sign: Aries
Siblings: None
Favourite TV show: *Friends* and *Star Trek: Voyager*
Favourite film: *The Matrix* and *The Fifth Element*
Favourite sweets: Fizzy cola bottles
Most romantic thing he's ever done: When he was about nine he saved up all his pocket money to buy the girl down the road he had a crush on chocolates and roses for Valentines Day. He even sent her a letter saying he loved her
Favourite flavour of crisps: Turkey and Stuffing, Bovril, or Beef and Onion
Favourite Blue song: 'All Rise'
First single ever bought: 'I Should Be So Lucky' by Kylie Minogue
Favourite catchphrase: 'In a bit' or 'spinning out'

→ Antony

Full name: Antony Daniel Costa
DOB: 23/6/1981
Height: 5' 8"
From: Edgware, Middlesex
Hair: Dark Brown / Black
Eyes: Dark Brown
Star sign: Cancer
Siblings: One brother and one sister
Favourite TV show: *Only Fools and Horses*
Favourite film: *Grease*
Favourite sweets: Fizzy cola bottles
Most romantic thing he's ever done: He once bought a girl after dinner mints and spent his last pennies getting the bus to take them to her
Favourite flavour of crisps: Smoky Bacon
Favourite Blue song: 'All Rise'
First single ever bought: 'Pray' by Take That
Favourite catchphrase: 'I would' and 'bothered'

➔ Simon

Full name: Simon Solomon Webbe
DOB: 30/3/1979
Height: 5' 10"
From: Manchester
Hair: Black
Eyes: Brown
Star sign: Aries
Siblings: Four brothers and two sisters
Favourite TV show: *Friends* and *Smallville*
Favourite film: *Belly*, a gangster film starring DMX, Nas and T-Boz.
Favourite sweets: Fizzy cola bottles
Most romantic thing he's ever done: Is always doing romantic things and says he falls in love daily!
Favourite flavour of crisps: Prawn Cocktail
Favourite Blue song: 'Long Time'
First single ever bought: 'Yo Sweetness' or 'I Pray', by MC Hammer.
Favourite catch phrase: 'I do' or 'I would'

One Love Album Launch Signing

Lee: This was in HMV in Oxford Street.

Simon: We had a really good turn out, and all our usual Blue faithfuls turned out, which is always nice. They're always there to support us.

Lee: One girl asked for my chewing gum. Did I give it to her? Yes!

Dunk: I signed a lot of breasts that day. We always get asked to sign breasts.

Ant: We were so pleased with the *One Love* album. We worked really hard on it and it was worth it. We're really proud of it.

A Brand New Album
Released 04.11.02

One Love Tour Announcement

Ant: This is when we announced that we were doing the One Love tour.

Dunk: We were sponsored by Acuvue contact lenses because they reckoned we had the most stopping power and we're all wearing them in the photos.

Ant: That was a great event because people like *London Tonight* and The Disney Channel and Nickelodeon came down.

Simon: And most importantly, the fans came down to support us.

Dunk: It was in an art gallery in Battersea in September.

Ant: They were filming an advert for the London Congestion Charge outside, so Bob Mills was there and we were watching him doing his thing.

Simon: I was growing my hair, which is why I'm wearing a bandana. My hair wasn't looking too good. I wore them pretty much the whole time I was growing my hair if it looked bad.

Ant: I look a bit chubby in these pictures. We totally slimmed down on the tour.

Dunk: We all look chunkier here actually, because we lost a lot of weight on the tour because it was so physical.

Lee: I lost weight on the tour but I also put a lot on, if you know what I mean. I lost a lot of fat, but I was working out so I built up muscle. I felt fit, though. I think it was the fittest I've ever been in my life!

blue
one love
ACUVUE 2
COLOURS
CONTACT LENSES

Horosopes

We've unlocked the secrets of the lads' star signs to find out what they reveal about the fantastic foursome.

Simon and Duncan – Aries – Fire Sign

Aries are outgoing and enthusiastic about everything they do. They have a strong spirit of adventure and if there's something new to be tried, they like to give it a go! They are brave and like to lead a crowd, and are always the centre of attention.

Aries like a challenge, and tend to be very sure of themselves. They stand up for what they believe in and always have strong opinions where it matters. They will never agree with someone for the sake of it, and like their opinions to be respected. However, they can be impatient and like to know that everything is in order in every situation. There's trouble if things aren't exactly as they should be!

Once they set their mind on something, they go for it whatever, especially when it comes to love. Because they are strong characters, they like being with a partner who is equally strong so that they've got someone to turn to in their hour of need. They need to know that someone is always there for them, and being trustworthy is a massive issue for them.

They are very romantic and like everything in a relationship to be as exciting and intense as possible. They tend to rush into relationships quickly and can fall in love easily, and because of this they are prone to getting hurt.

That said, once Aries do find their perfect match they are incredibly loyal and very giving and faithful. But on the down side, they can be a bit selfish if they're not getting their own way and tend to overcomplicate matters. They like to feel very special in a relationship, so their ideal partner has to be someone who is as giving and loyal as they are and also shares their lust for life.

When it comes to friends, again Aries are loyal to people they care about. However, if anyone upsets them a row will be just around the corner! They are quick to argue and will always stand up for themselves. But once the argument is over, they swiftly forgive and forget and will happily act as if nothing has happened.

Work-wise, Aries like to get noticed and not surprisingly they are great entertainers. Their leadership skills are a bonus in any job, and while they can occasionally be difficult to work alongside because of their bossy streak, they are also hard working and dedicated to whatever they do.

Ant – Cancer - Water Sign

Cancerians are sensitive souls and can be very emotional, but they're certainly no pushover! They love nature and the world around them, but sometimes find that life gets a bit stressful at times. They are extremely protective of their families and always want to make sure they are okay. And even though friends are very important to them, family are their prime concern and they're constantly looking out for them.

For this reason a secure home life is incredibly important to Cancerians and they hate to feel that their home is being invaded or is under threat in any way. They can be very strong willed when they need to be, so when it comes to matters of the home they are not ones to cross!

Cancerians are determined and have a touch of selfishness about them, they can also be a little self-pitying if the mood takes them. But ultimately they are very loving and will always go out their way to help people and make them feel comfortable.

When it comes to love, they are easy going and easy to get along with, but don't fall for people easily. They have a fear of rejection, so they always make sure that a potential partner likes them before they turn on the charm. However, when they want to commit, they really go for it and nothing can hold back their romantic mood.

They're not always the easiest people to date as they can be moody, but they are one hundred percent devoted, kind, and reliable.
As a friend, you couldn't ask for better than a Cancerian. They are cautious when it comes to meeting new people, but once they meet someone they like they'll be your friend for life and will always be there for you. But be warned - they expect the same high level of devotion and trust from friends as they give.

Work-wise, Cancerians like to know that their work is secure and they panic if the slightest thing goes wrong. They tend to worry about money a lot, so they like to know that they are always looked after financially.

They are very practical and down to earth, which stands them in good stead whatever their occupation, and are willing to work hard to get to the top of their game.

Lee - Gemini – Air Sign

Gemini are always jumping from one thing to another and are constantly intrigued by what's going on in the world. They are keen to learn, and no stone is left unturned if they are trying to find out about something. They are curious and fascinated by the smallest thing, and always willing to take a risk if it means they will find the answer to a question.

They find it difficult to settle down to one thing and have a million different things on their mind at any one time. This is often why they don't hear you when you talk to them – there's too much else going on in their mind for them to even notice!

They have a love of life and it is important to them that everyone understands their point of view. They will happily talk for days on the same subject just to get their message across.

Where love is concerned, they need someone who is happy to listen to their musings and will be patient with them. In return, they are generous with their feelings, extremely kind, and always willing to listen to others.

They like to shop around when it comes to love, but when they fall for someone, they fall hard, and find it very hard to get over lost loves. They like to have someone around to fall back on, and get very frustrated if things don't work out as they are idealists.

Gemini are brilliant friends to have as they're trustworthy and can be extremely entertaining. They are fun and optimistic and because they can charm the birds off the trees they often have many friends, but trust very few due to their suspicious nature.

They've always got brilliant ideas for things to do and are always happy to try anything new, no matter how wild. Although they can be very indecisive at times, they are good communicators and suit just about any job that involves talking. Creative jobs are also ideal for them, although they're not likely to stick at one thing for very long!

Turning on the Oxford Street Christmas Lights

Simon: This was a brilliant night - and we got 20% discount at the store! I went in there and bought a coat. I didn't feel like I was properly dressed for the occasion, so I went around buying clothes with my discount. It was great.

Lee: We all did a bit of shopping. It was freezing and none of us had enough clothes on so we went on a bit of a spending spree. That was a laugh.

Ant: It was a cool event and an amazing thing to do. People like Ronan Keating, S Club and Spice Girls have all done it, so to be asked to do it in front of everyone was brilliant.

Simon: It was an honour.

Dunk: It was mad because we got up into the box to actually turn on the lights and we realised how many people there were there. There were so, so many. We couldn't believe how many people had turned up. The street was totally packed.

Ant: There were about twenty thousand people there!

Simon: The Oxford Street Christmas lights are one of those things where when you're a kid and you come to London you look at the lights and wonder how they turn them on. When I used to come to London with my mum I used to stare at them for ages, so it was mad that we were the ones bringing it all to life.

Lee: It was an amazing event and it was an honour to be there in front of all those people. I remember seeing the Spice Girls doing it years ago and thinking it was such a big deal. It was an amazing experience. But everything we do is an amazing experience. Do you know what I mean? The way I see it, we've turned on the Oxford Street lights, and even if we never do it again we'll remember that time for the rest of or lives.

Ant: I think we all look really different in this picture. It's weird to look back and see how much we've changed and how much we've come on. It's mad.

Top of the Pops Awards/Disney Awards

Top of the Pops

Lee: This was a really good day. We had all the dancers with us for the first time and the show was wicked.

Simon: We walked through the crowd surrounded by bouncers and it felt so good.

Lee: We won Best Pop Act there.

Ant: The fans voted for it so it was a massive boost for us. We performed 'Fly By' on the show, which went down really well.

Simon: And I got to do the speech because the awards were in my hometown of Manchester.

Ant: We were in really high spirits and partied on the tour bus on the way home.

Simon: I didn't, though. They all went back and I stayed and I got accused of snogging this actress when all I was doing was talking to her! That sort of thing happens all the time. It's crazy.

Disney Awards

Ant: We won Best Pop Act at the Disney Awards as well.

Dunk: We've won a lot of awards. It's weird when you sit back and think about it. It's really cool, but we don't take winning awards for granted.

Simon: Whenever we win something it feels good and it's really appreciated, no matter what category it is. Even to be nominated is cool. And if the awards are voted for by the fans, they mean even more to us.

Channel
Kids
NE LOV
PUMA

In the Stars for Blue!

If only you had a crystal ball and could look into the future to find out exactly when you're going to settle down with the Blue boy of your choice. Well sadly we can't predict that, but our psychic, Astro Annie, has looked into what's in store for 2004.

Lee • Gemini • Air Sign

In the first six months of 2004, Gemini will grow and change emotionally, but in a very positive way. As a Gemini, Lee learns from all his experiences and even when it seems that he's not noticing what's going on around him, he will be taking everything in.

From the beginning of the summer onwards Lee can look forward to an upturn in his fortunes and will get an unexpected windfall around August time. But he also has to be careful as something he's been neglecting may come back to haunt him around the same time, and he will need to address the situation once and for all. Once he does, he'll realise that it wasn't nearly as stressful as he first thought.

Socially, from the summer up until the middle of autumn will be a fantastic time for Gemini. Romance is also in the air and it's entirely possible that Lee will meet a special lady around this time, although it may be some time before anything really solid happens as it will be quite difficult to get the relationship off the ground. A former love will also come back into his life, and he will have to make a tough decision, but it will be the right one. Gemini have a certain charm which attracts people to them, and Lee will find that his attractiveness is at an all time high towards the end of the year. But he will definitely be concentrating his energies on one person for a while.

Lee will round the year off feeling upbeat and excited about future projects. He will receive a work offer from someone, which will surprise and excite him, and it will set him up for a hectic year to come. Christmas will be a time of reflection for Gemini as they sit back and take a look at what they've achieved over the past year. They will also appreciate the company of friends and family around this time and Lee will see it as a time to relax and build himself up for a busy but productive 2005!

Dunk and Simon • Aries • Fire sign

2004 was always going to be quite a challenging time for Aries, and the first few months will make for a mixture of emotions. But they've held up well to the challenges of an eventful 2003 and will continue working hard to make their dreams a reality.

After a slow start, February sees Aries feeling positive and looking forward, and this includes making solid plans for the future. It's likely that Simon and Dunk will start thinking quite far ahead and working out what they really want from life.

March and April will probably be quite manic and leave them feeling a bit overwhelmed, but from May onwards things will start to settle down and they will feel more in control again.

The summer months will be a light-hearted, fun time for Dunk and Simon, but will not be without periods of hard work! They will go through a phase in the summer months where more will be expected of them than ever before and there will be a couple of moments of panic, but they'll be surprised how well they deal with it and it will make them feel much stronger and happier in the long run.

Romance is in the air throughout June, July and August, and both boys will find they aren't short of female company! Towards the end of summer, they will make the most of the opportunity to party and have a laugh, including some romantic interest. It's unlikely to be a life partner for Aries, but it will certainly be a lot of fun!

Autumn will bring new responsibilities and some exciting news for Aries that they weren't expecting. The dull weather at the beginning of Autumn will make the pair feel like hibernating, but by November they will have much more energy and be at their peak in the run up to Christmas.

The New Year will get off to a flying start with a few more surprises rearing their heads, and an offer from abroad will see Dunk and Simon in very high spirits and provides much excitement in 2005!

Ant • Cancer • Water sign

Cancerians will start 2004 as they mean to go on – feeling revived and ready for whatever comes their way. January may not be the easiest of months for level headed Ant, but he won't let things get him down and huge improvements will be on the way.

The next few months will prove to be a mixture of hard work and enjoyment, and it's likely Cancerians will be in good spirits and excited about upcoming events, and Ant will be in a positive frame of mind. May brings an unsettled time which will leave calm Cancerians feeling a little out of their depth, but it will quickly be resolved and events will take a turn for the better.

The summer will be a time for fun and Ant will have a lot of love and support around him. It's also going to be an amazing time for love with everything falling into place and the sun making him feel more romantic than ever.

Ant needs to be careful about giving himself a hard time as autumn creeps in. He may feel a bit lacking in motivation, leading he and other Cancerians to spend some time on their own to reflect on what's been going on around them. As soon as October clears though, things will be back on track and new, exciting changes will be on the cards.

Life will become more exciting than ever in November and it'll be a great chance for Ant to socialise and catch up with old friends. A big party or gathering towards the end of November will leave Cancerians feeling very happy and satisfied with life!

The 2002 Tour

Tell us about the your 2002 tour…

Ant: The tour was the most incredible experience. The best thing for us was performing in front of all the fans.

Lee: It was so amazing and I can't wait to do it again, but it is hard work and it's a strain on your vocal chords. My throat gave out one day because I left the air conditioning on in my hotel room overnight. I got up the next morning and my voice had had it. We had to be really careful.

Simon: We had some wicked outfits. The first outfits and the 70s outfits were my favourites, then the Bounce outfits, then the 'Fly By' ones.

Whose idea were the 70s outfits?

Ant: It was our idea to do a 70s medley, but our stylist Caroline made the outfits. She's the best.

Dunk: It was wicked. I had flares that she altered to make them extra big. I love the 70s anyway so I thought it looked so cool.

Lee: The 70s outfits were wicked. Everyone loved them. I really enjoyed them because they were different. I became a different person when I was wearing the 70s gear and as soon as I put the outfit on I went into character. The 'Riders' outfits were wicked as well. They were really blinging. I loved the whole show. I love watching it back and seeing what we did. I think I'll watch it before we go off on tour again to get myself ready.

Dunk: I love the picture where we're all doing different things. It looks wicked and kind of sums up the tour.

Lee: I don't think I've got a best bit of the tour, I think the whole thing was brilliant. I liked singing 'If You Come Back' the most, and also 'Riders'. It was the opening song and I don't think people expected us to come out dancing. A lot of people said how wicked it was because they didn't expect the gig to be like it was. It was a real show. Loads of people said to me that they thought it would be like an r'n'b concert, but it was more like a proper 'show' show and there was a lot to it. That's what we're about. We don't try to be cool, we like to go mad and go for it.

Did you do the whole rock'n'roll party thing on tour?

Ant: We didn't actually have that many parties on the tour. We're pretty strict and we don't drink alcohol when we're performing.

Simon: Also, by the time you come off stage you're shattered, especially if you're doing two shows in a day. After that all you want to do is go back to your hotel room and relax. We were on stage for two hours at a time, which is really full-on.

Dunk: We did go to the hotel bars quite a lot with the dancers and sit around and have drinks, but we never went mad and went out. We just wouldn't have been able to do it. We needed to save our energy.

Lee: I was really good. I was good when we went on the Smash Hits tour as well. I won the 'Most Boring' award on the Smash Hits tour because I used to go to bed early. I don't go out a lot, but every time I do I get into the papers for being stupid or getting chucked out of somewhere or something, so everyone assumes I go out all the time. But I'm more of a stay at home kind of guy and I'm more dedicated to the music than anything. If I do let my hair down then I really go for it, but it's not all that often. We had a couple of good nights out on the tour but we did have to look after our throats. I'd ruin my voice if I went out all the time.

Ant: We did have one night out, but we went to see James Bond at the cinema so it wasn't that rock'n'roll!

Dunk: And I went to see Harry Potter instead!

Which celebs came to check out the show?

Ant: Quite a lot of celebrities came to see the tour. Dawn French, Kate Lawler, Dale Winton, Shane Richie…

Lee: Dani Behr, some of the Royals…

Dunk: Yes, Fergie and the kids, The Beckhams with their kids, Heidi from the Sugababes…

Simon: Ryan Giggs came, One True Voice…

Ant: All our friends and family came as well, which meant a lot to us.

Lee: All my mates came to the show. They loved it.

Simon, your band VS were performing. How did they get on?

Simon: They were wicked. It was so nice watching them perform just before we went on stage. They bought me close to tears and stuff a few times.

Dunk: This one time me and Si were hidden behind this drinks machine watching VS, and a couple of people came to the bar and did a double take because Si and I were crawling out from behind this drinks machine. We were sneakily watching them perform and people were really shocked to see us hiding away.

Which song went down best with the crowd?

Ant: Probably 'All Rise'.

Simon: But it's hard to tell because it was so loud all the way through. I think they all went down well. There was a lot more stuff that we wanted to do on the tour, but there just wasn't the time. We'll have to do it all on the next tour.

Lee: I think all the songs went down well as well. They all had different vibes and people got into all of them. There's nothing better than looking at the audience and knowing they're loving what you're doing. It's such a buzz. The good thing about the band is that we're all so different, so we all bring something different to a live show. We're not just standing there sticking to a routine and doing what's expected of us. We all do our own thing.

Did anyone fall over or do anything dodgy or make a fool of themselves?

Dunk: Yes, cameramen fell over and all sorts. This one night everything that could go wrong did, but thankfully it was only one night.

Lee: When you're on that stage you can do anything and there are no boundaries. You've got so much energy and it's all your own interpretation of the music and you do what comes naturally to you. So if you do anything silly, you don't mind. Some groups go out there and they're so choreographed that they're all doing the same thing over and over again every night. We don't do that.

Dunk: We do like to get out there and go mad. We always let ourselves go. You really can't help it.

First night of the tour

Lee: This was in Dublin at The Point and we were kicking off the tour. Dublin is a wicked place.

Ant: I was really nervous the first night, and that was the night when everything went wrong!

Dunk: A cameraman fell down a hole in the stage…

Simon: The car we used on the show broke down on the first night as well.

Lee: And my foot almost got trapped in the trap door…

Dunk: …so everything that could have gone wrong did go wrong, but thankfully things did improve and it was an incredible tour. Teething problems happen to all new bands on tour, its all just part of the business.

Follow The Path To True Blue Love

All of the boys in Blue were blessed in the looks, personality and talent departments, so it's hard not to love them all! So we've made it easier for you to find which Blue boy you're best suited to with our Path to True Blue Love...

Start Here

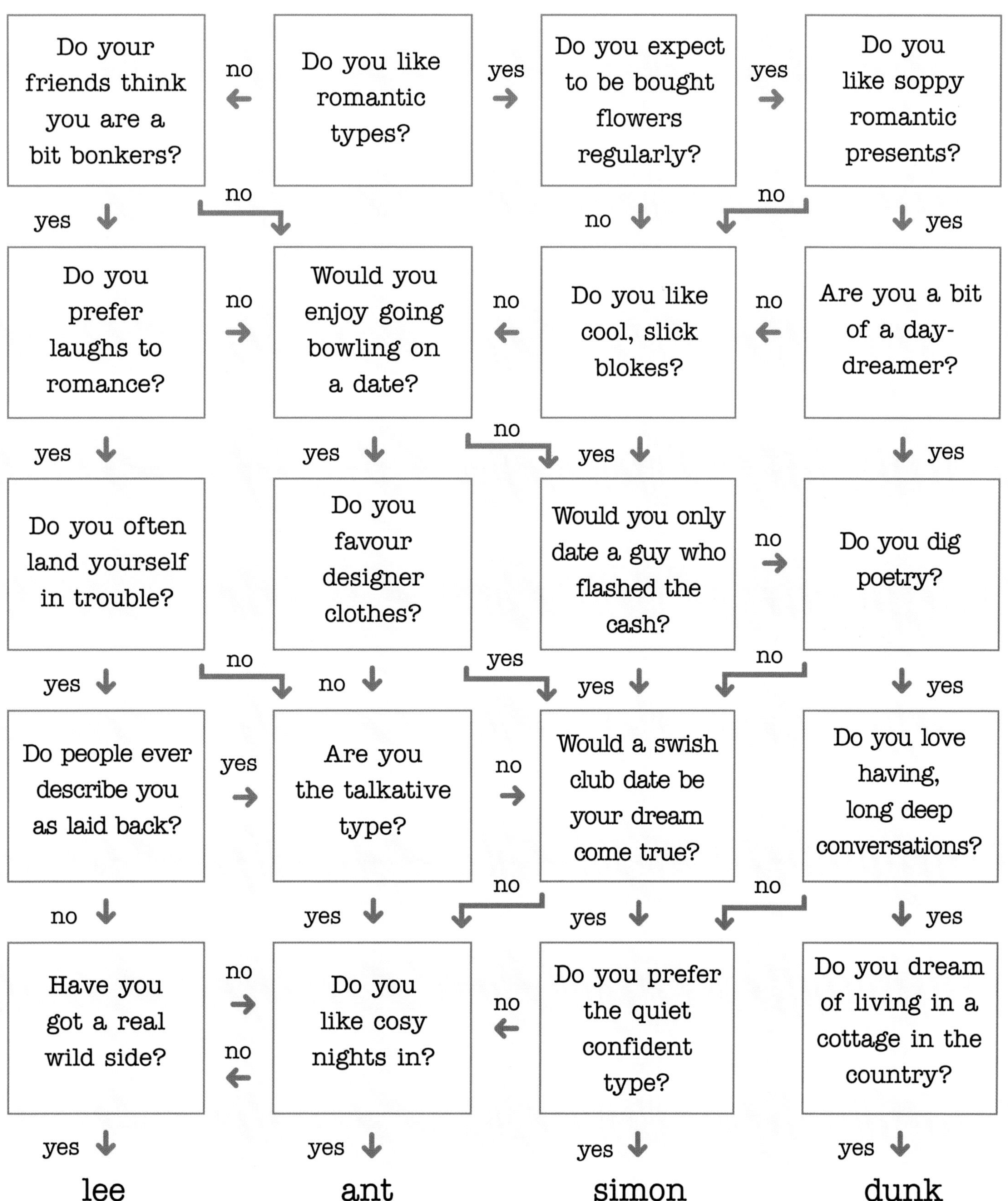
Do your friends think you are a bit bonkers?
no
Do you like romantic types?
yes
Do you expect to be bought flowers regularly?
yes
Do you like soppy romantic presents?
yes
no
no
no
yes
Do you prefer laughs to romance?
no
Would you enjoy going bowling on a date?
no
Do you like cool, slick blokes?
no
Are you a bit of a day-dreamer?
yes
yes
no
yes
yes
Do you often land yourself in trouble?
Do you favour designer clothes?
Would you only date a guy who flashed the cash?
no
Do you dig poetry?
yes
no
no
yes
yes
no
yes
Do people ever describe you as laid back?
yes
Are you the talkative type?
no
Would a swish club date be your dream come true?
Do you love having, long deep conversations?
no
yes
no
yes
no
yes
Have you got a real wild side?
no
no
Do you like cosy nights in?
no
Do you prefer the quiet confident type?
Do you dream of living in a cottage in the country?
yes
lee
yes
ant
yes
simon
yes
dunk

Performing with Elton John

How did the Elton John duet on 'Sorry Seems To Be The Hardest Word' come about?

Dunk: It was Lee's idea, and we were all big fans of Elton anyway.

Lee: I'd always loved the song, and the record company approached Elton to see if he wanted to play piano on the track.

Dunk: And Elton basically said: 'Yes, of course I'd love to do that, and I'd like to sing on it as well'. It was amazing. And at first he couldn't do the video because he was too busy, but we spoke to him at an awards ceremony and sang with him on stage, and he agreed to do it after that, which was brilliant. We were so pleased.

Did you enjoy doing Children in Need with Elton too?

Ant: This was the day before we did our first gig in Minehead, so we had dress rehearsals in the afternoon, then we had to be back in London to do *Children In Need* in the evening. We got a helicopter there and back, so we were pretty tired by the end of the night.

Simon: It was really cool, though. It was quite mad being flown in especially for a gig. It was the first time it had happened.

Lee: Do you know what, that's rock'n'roll, that is. I loved that. It's what makes this job fun. We were nearly late for the show, though, because everything was so rushed. It was a close call.

Ant: It was great performing with Elton as well. He's a good lad.

Have you ever been to Elton's house? Everyone says it's amazing...

Lee: Yes, we went to the one in Windsor and it's incredible.

Simon: We actually saw it when we were flying to Minehead in the helicopter that time. We had a bird's eye view and saw how his garden paths light up. Its amazing!

Lee: Elton John's party was one of my biggest dreams come true. We got up and sang and it was the first time we'd ever sung with Elton John. It's something I'll never, ever forget. It was just amazing.

Elton John's Charity Aution

Lee: This suit cost me a fortune, and so many people have asked me why I spent so much money on it. I've got two reasons. One, it was for charity, and two, it was sentimental to me. It's something I can keep forever. Elton is a legend and it's like owning something of Michael Jackson's or Frank Sinatra's. So to have something that he's actually worn and owned and performed in... It was something I couldn't pass up. I chose that particular suit because it was the best one they had in there. I asked them for the best one, and I was lucky I got it. Well actually I haven't got it yet, I'm still waiting for it to be delivered. But I can't wait to actually have it!

The Brits

Simon: This was our second BRITs and this time we got to perform, which was amazing. We performed our 'Riders' routine from the tour mixed in with a little bit of 'One Love'. And then we actually won an award for Best Pop Act. We were up against Will, Gareth, Pink and The Sugababes so it was a tough category, and we were well pleased to win.

Ant: All awards are brilliant, but to win a BRIT award is incredible because they're so prestigious.

Simon: When we did our acceptance speech we thanked everyone including the record company, management, family, and most of all the fans. The fans mean the world to us.

Did you have any idea that you were going to win the award?

Simon: No. In fact, we didn't think we had. They blagged it because they had the cameras over by Will and Gareth so it looked like one of them had won, then suddenly the cameras came rushing towards us.

Dunk: We were all whispering to each other going: 'We haven't got it, the cameras are over there' then the cameras swung round on us and we were stunned. All you saw on camera was Antony jumping up and going mad. It was wicked.

How did you decide what song you would perform at the BRITs?

Simon: We decided collectively. We wanted something with a bit of energy and we didn't have a lot of time to rehearse, so it made sense to do something from the tour. It was pretty manic because we had sixteen dancers, so there were twenty of us on stage. But we were really pleased with how it went.

Who was the biggest partier out of you all on BRITs night?

Dunk: We all partied hard, it was a wicked night.

Simon: I can't remember much about the BRITs to be honest. We went mad!

Ant: We were up until about four the next morning. It was the first time we'd all been out partying together in ages, so we made the most of it.

Lee: It was amazing. It was such a top night.

Overheard!

Okay, so you think you know the Blue boys inside out, but can you pick out who said what from this little lot? Check out the following quotes and see if you can spot who said what!

01 'I was very disappointed because I'm usually the party animal and no one can beat me, but they did.'

02 'I used to snog girls behind the curtains at school discos.

03 'I hate posing. I know you have to sometimes but I hate doing it, I'm not a big poseur.'

04 'I'm always the first to get ready. It takes me about twenty minutes.'

05 'I don't go to that many parties. I'm a bit of a boring git.'

06 'I've met all the people I've really wanted to meet.'

07 'I'd like a part in Friends. I'd be Monica's guy because I like her dark hair.'

08 'I'd like to appear on *Who Wants To Be A Millionaire*. I'd like to see Chris Tarrant's eyes up close and feel all the tension.'

09 'I used to phone fans up to say hello and say thanks for their letters. They were always a bit shocked!'

10 'We used to go to parties as teenagers and spill things on the carpet and break things. Something always went wrong.'

11 'This girl once stood in front of me and started screaming and saying she couldn't believe she was touching me. I suddenly thought, "she thinks I'm famous". It was weird.'

12 'If you're having fun and getting on that's the most important thing. That's so romantic.'

13 'When the audience is screaming for some reason, sometimes it makes me want to be back in their shoes dreaming of being up there on stage.'

14 'If things don't change, they stay as they are.'

15 'I want to name my kids something to do with the world. Something that's quite strong.'

16 'I look at girls and think: "You could be my wife".'

17 'I can chew my toenails.'

How many did you get right?

1-6

Feeling Blue? Oh dear, you're not too good at spotting the lads' speak are you? Get reading more interviews in order to improve your quote spotting skills!

7-12

Hmm, not too bad, but you could do with brushing up on your Blue speak. You're obviously a big fan, but need to get to know the lads that little bit better!

13 - 17

You could recognise a Blue quote at a hundred paces and are obviously a 100% true Blue fan. We salute you, top quote spotter!

Answers

01 Ant
02 Duncan
03 Lee
04 Ant
05 Lee
06 Simon
07 Simon
08 Ant
09 Lee
10 Simon
11 Ant
12 Duncan
13 Simon
14 Ant
15 Lee
16 Simon
17 Lee

Highlights from the Blue Calendar

Smash Hits Tour

Lee: This picture was taken on the Smash Hits tour in Sheffield in 2002. We only got to do one gig because we had our own tour, which was a real shame because we had such a wicked time the year before.

Ant: We were the partying ringleaders in 2001 and we were up every night. All Stars, Liberty X and Atomic Kitten were on the tour as well, and we had such a laugh every night.

Lee: Apart from me. I was a bit boring as I mentioned before.

Donny Osmond Show

Dunk: *The Donny Osmond Show* was funny. There were loads of celebrities there and Donny was such a nice guy.

Simon: He sung 'One Love' with us and I got to ask him a question, which was, 'Have you ever thought of reuniting with your brothers and doing a one-off concert?' and hey presto, his brothers appeared on stage!

Ant: My mum got up on stage as well. She loves Donny and she though it was fantastic.

Is there really any rivalry between you and Westlife?

Ant: No, we love them, man.

Simon: I think the rivalry was down to a lot of press. I think it also might be a bit of a fan thing because people think that you can't like Westlife and Blue. But we're mates and have got no problem with each other at all. I've got a lot of respect for those boys.

Which other pop bands are you mates with?

Dunk: The Sugababes are cool, Liberty X are really nice people, and the Mis-teeq girls are cool too.

Simon: It's not like we're all in each other phones books and go out for dinner all the time, but we do get on.

GABBAN
Authentic

GABBANA DOLCE & GABBANA
DOLCE & GABBANA DOLCE

Which Blue Gang Would You Be In?

Everyone has a favourite Blue boy, but do you know which one you'd get on best with if you were hanging out together? Take our revealing quiz to discover which Blue gang you should join!

01 What would be your ideal way to spend a Saturday?
a Doing something energetic and fun like paint balling
b Lying in the sun daydreaming about the object of your affection
c Shopping 'till you drop
d Hanging out with your mates in the park having a laugh

02 Where would your ideal date be?
a Anywhere you can dance and have a laugh
b A romantic candle lit restaurant
c Somewhere chic where you could really dress up
d A lively restaurant with a brilliant atmosphere

03 What would you most like to be given for your next birthday?
a A flying lesson
b A huge stuffed toy
c A pair of cool sunglasses
d A really cool pair of jeans

04 What's your duvet like?
a Bright and fun
b Light coloured with a slight pattern
c Cool and plain
d Football themed

05 How would you describe your personality?
a A laugh and up for anything
b A cheerful romantic
c Cool and friendly
d Laid back and very likeable

06 What are you most likely to get told off for at school?
a Being cheeky to your teacher
b Daydreaming
c Wearing sunglasses in class
d Laughing with your mates

07 When it comes to your hair, do you…

a Keep it in pretty much the same style most of the time
b Have a certain style but like to experiment
c Always try different things
d Like to keep it looking good but don't fuss over it

08 Which is your favourite out of these school subjects?

a Music
b English
c PE
d Drama

09 Which of these is your favourite Blue song?

a All Rise
b If You Come Back
c One Love
d You Make Me Wanna

Now count up how many a's, b's, c's or d's you've got and check out who you'd get on best with!

Mostly a's
You should be in lively Lee's gang! You're always up for a laugh and like trying anything a bit different. You're popular, creative and fun, and always at the centre of any party.

Mostly b's
You'd be in romantic Duncan's gang! You're very much led by your heart and while you love being with people and having a laugh, you need time out on your own to chill and have a think sometimes.

Mostly c's
You should be in cool Si's gang! You're known as the hip one among your mates, and people are always seeking fashion advice from you. You're popular and a good talker, and always get invited to the best parties.

Mostly d's
You should be in laid-back Ant's gang! You're funny and cheerful can get along with everyone, and even your teachers like you. But you also have a lovely sensitive side and are good at dealing with other people's problems.

Clothes Show Live

Ant: Modelling at the Clothes Show Live was weird, man. I felt really self-conscious because I'd never done anything like that before.

Simon: For me it was a blast from the past. It was nice to go back and do the catwalk as a celebrity. It made the fact that I'd done modelling before worthwhile. That's why I did the modelling - as a way to get into music - and it paid off.

Dunk: I found modelling quite strange. It was kind of surreal. At first I thought 'What are we doing?' but then we got into it and took it as a laugh. Vernon Kay and June Sarpong from T4 were presenting so we were up on stage with them and we had a giggle.

Lee: It was cool, but I did feel weird doing it at first. I felt weird standing there and having all these people looking at me when I wasn't singing or anything.

Ant: You have to walk all the way up and have your picture taken before you walk back, and you have to stand there while people stare at you. It felt so strange.

Dunk: But Simon helped us by giving us advice. He just said to us to relax and enjoy it and it'll be all-good. And in the end we did enjoy it, especially when we all pulled our pants down and did a moonie when we walked off at the end!

ENYCE

It's been a whirlwind year

MTV Asia Awards

Ant: We did the MTV Asia awards just after Christmas. It was a really busy and manic, but we did alright. We won Best Pop Act there and beat the likes of Enrique Englasias and No Doubt – people that have been around for a few years - so that felt good.

Lee: It's quite frenzied in Asia but the fans are really friendly and give you nice presents. They're always really polite and ask you how you are and write you nice poems and stuff. They're incredibly dedicated.

Duncan on Blind Date

Dunk: I had giggle on *Blind Date* and ended up going on a little holiday to Barcelona with Sally, the girl who picked me. The camera crew were really laid back and nice and we had a lot of time on our own to chat and get to know each other. We had big apartments in this really nice hotel, and Sally and me had interconnecting doors. Did I snog her? Yes I did, just to say thanks for coming away with me! We're still in touch and I spoke to her earlier today, actually. She was in Italy as she's gone away travelling. I got a phone call from Cilla last week as well. She calls up every now and again and says: 'Alright chuck?' Cilla's lovely.

Ant and girlfriend Lucy

Ant: I proposed to Lucy the day after this year's BRIT awards. I'm so happy, and all the fans have been great about her and really supportive, so I want to say thanks. They all really like her. She's a great girl so it's hard not to.
We do get photographed when we're out and about every now and again but I don't mind.

Your Song
Antony
Duncan
one love
Simon

Discography

Albums

All Rise

May 2001 – No.1

One Love

November 2001 – No.1

Singles

All Rise

May 2001 – No.4

Too Close

August 2001 – No.1

If You Come Back

November 2001 – No.1

Fly By

March 2002 – No.6

One Love

October 2002 – No.3

Sorry Seems To Be The Hardest Word

December 2002 – No.1

You Make Me Wanna

March 2003 – No.4

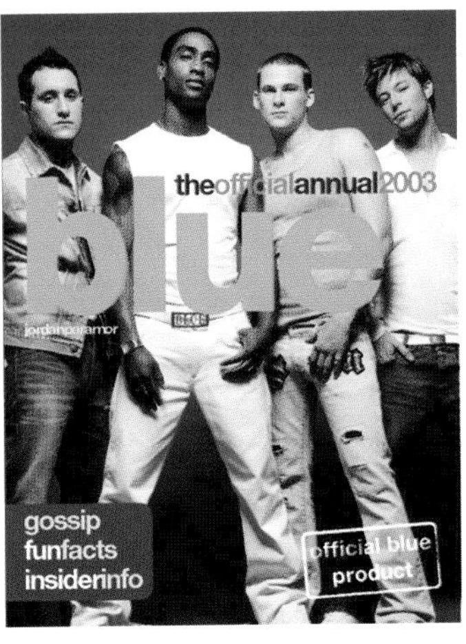

Books

All Rise

April 2002

Official Blue Annual

August 2002

Blue on Blue

October 2002 (HB)

May 2003 (PB)

On the Road with Blue

November 2003

Official Blue Fan Club

Proprietors: Fiona and Andrea (Dunk and Ants' mums)
To become a member of our fan club all you need to do is drop us a line with SAE requesting a form or visit our website.
You can be an Official member, a Social member or a VIP member

Official Membership: - £10 per year
One year's membership / Exclusive Official Blue Fan Club, interactive multimedia CD (as standard) worth £12.99. (Or funky shiny black OBFC bag if you do not have a computer) / Membership ID number / 10% discount on all Official Blue Fan Club Merchandise / Exclusive access to Members' Area - includes message board, newsletters, ticket allocations, updates on gigs and much more / Quarterly Newsletter

Social Membership: - £17.50 per year
Social membership offers everything tha the Official membership offers plus exclusive access to OBFChat. OBFChat is an exclusive 3D chat environment that allows you to chat in real time to other OBFC members.

VIP Membership: - £25 per year
This is our top of the range, exclusive membership, which includes all the benefits that the other memberships have to offer plus your very own BLUEmail account.

(Payment can be made using a debit/credit card online www.officialbluefanclub.com or by cheque/postal order by post)

Official Blue Fan Club
PO Box 5329, Wimborne BH21 4XN
Telephone your order on: **01202 598738**
(Mon-Fri 8.45am-6.00pm)
Or join on Line:
join@officialbluefanclub.com
We invite you to visit our wicked funky website: **www.officialbluefanclub.com**

BOSS